BLACK MATTERS

Afua Cooper
Wilfried Raussert

Roseway Publishing
An imprint of Fernwood Publishing
Halifax & Winnipeg

Authors: Afua Cooper and Wilfried Raussert
Editor: Fazeela Jiwa
Design: LOKI

Printed and bound in Canada

 Published by Roseway Publishing
an imprint of Fernwood Publishing

32 Oceanvista Lane, Black Point,
Nova Scotia, B0J 1B0
and 748 Broadway Avenue, Winnipeg,
Manitoba, R3G 0X3
www.fernwoodpublishing.ca/roseway

Fernwood Publishing Company Limited
gratefully acknowledges the financial support
of the Government of Canada through the
Canada Book Fund, the Canada Council for the
Arts, the Province of Nova Scotia, Arts Nova
Scotia, and the Province of Manitoba for our
publishing program. For the production of
this book, we acknowledge the support of the
German Federal Ministry of Education
and Research.

Library and Archives Canada Cataloguing
in Publication

Title: Black matters / Afua Cooper ;
[photographs by] Wilfried Raussert.
Names: Cooper, Afua, author. | Raussert,
Wilfried, photographer.
Description: Poems.
Identifiers: Canadiana 2020030562X |
ISBN 9781773632957 (softcover)
Classification: LCC PS8555.O584 B53 2020 |
DDC C811/.54—dc23

I thank wholeheartedly Wilfried Raussert, who proposed
this collaboration, for his photographs, images, and
enthusiastic partnership of art and poetry; Lamarana
Cooper Diallo (Lami), who travelled with me to many of
the places mentioned in the poems and served as muse
for poetry and photography; Habiba Cooper Diallo for her
encouragement and support as I worked on the manuscript
during the surreal context of COVID-19 devastations and
lockdown; Roseway Publishing for accepting the manuscript;
and Fazeela Jiwa, whose patient, respectful, thoughtful,
and enthusiastic editing made this work better.

—A.C.

I would like to thank Afua Cooper for a joyful collaboration
and for her inspiring poetry and vision. I thank also the
German Federal Ministry of Research and Education for
their financial support of this publication in the context
of the Entangled Americas project, sponsored by the German
institution for seven years between 2013 and 2019.[1]
Additionally, my sincere thanks to all the street artists for
making urban space social and communal. And further,
heartfelt thanks to Lamarana Cooper Diallo, Alina Munoz
Knudsen, Blessed Okosun, and Sigrid Yanara Castillo for
their kind cooperation. Finally, many thanks to the members
of the Black Americas network who provided a supportive
and critical community for projects joining arts and sciences.[2]

—W.R.

1. https://uni-bielefeld.de/cias/entangled_americas
2. https://uni-bielefeld.de/cias/blackamericas

This book is a dialogue between image and text. Wilfried Raussert is the photographer, Afua Cooper is the poet.

Resulting from numerous walks in cities of the Americas and Europe, the images capture the ubiquity of Black cultures and people. The African continent is powerfully present everywhere. While the images speak to the presence of Black people in contemporary societies, they often engage past historical and mythological epochs. The past and present comingle. Photographs, paintings, and murals express Black beauty and Black power in public space and everyday life — and the political importance of that presence. Beyond that, the images want to inspire poetic and narrative responses. The poems are inspired by the images, responding to them directly and indirectly. They give voice to Black beauty, power, and resistance in words and sound. At the same time, they inhabit a world of their own beyond and outside the images.

The collaboration between Wilfried Raussert and Afua Cooper was joyful and fruitful. It began in 2017 when the photographer shared his photos with the poet. Her response to them was to first engage in a deep reflection: observation and meditation. What is the photographer trying to say? What is the subject within the frame thinking? What myths, legends, histories, secrets, and tales are the images trying to express? What are they hiding?

"Father and Son," while a contemporary photograph, calls on the poet's historical memory to write "John Ware: Magician Cowboy" in honour of the legendary Albertan cowboy, John Ware. In the photo, a man strides confidently, holding his son in his arms. Both father and son are framed by shamanistic mementos (for example, the four directions) and by the symbol of cattle. As Ware was both a talented cowboy and a loving father, the poet asks, might this be a modern-day John Ware? The photo inspired the poem discussing Ware's early life as a slave, his flight to the West after the Civil War, his life in Canada, and his career as a cowboy and horseman. But who were his parents? From where did they come? The poet's imagination then took flight and travelled with Ware to ancient kingdoms in what are now Ghana and Nigeria.

The photo "Diversity, Toronto" is a collage of people of diverse "races" and genders. A Black man takes centre stage as he strides above the collage, in which there is no representation of Blackness. The image narrates a moment of Black empowerment and takes the poet into the past, as she meditates on what "diversity" meant in Toronto two hundred years ago. She encounters enslaved Black woman Peggy Pompadour, her husband, and her three children. The poem "Fugitive" tells the story of Peggy, who was owned by Upper Canadian elites Elizabeth and Peter Russell. Peggy's attempts to free herself and her children — Jupiter, Amy, and Milly — from bondage and reside as a Maroon on the outskirts of Toronto could be thought of as a practice of fugitivity, a condition that marks Black life in all locales, from slavery into present time. The diversity of twenty-first-century Toronto must be read against the bodies of its early inhabitants like Peggy Pompadour and her enslaved children.

The poem "Cimarron" also invokes the theme of marronage. A Black Mexican sells jewellery and other items on the streets of Granada, Spain, as he dodges Spanish immigration officials who track down illegal immigrants, migrants, gypsies, and other persons deemed undesirable. This cimarron invokes Yanga, the African Maroon who led an anti-slavery and anti-colonial war in seventeenth-century Mexico against Spanish slaveowners and colonizers. Fugitivity thus links the Black experience across time, space, and linguistic and colonial frontiers. The image chosen for this poem, "Black Americas," points to the ubiquity of the Maroon experience in the Americas.

Similar themes of slavery, flight, resistance, and resilience are also articulated in "Jupiter Wise." Jupiter, a slave from Prince Edward Island, ended up in court in 1786 for assault, and larceny. The poet imagines Jupiter not only as a runaway but also a jinn, the ultimate shapeshifter. To survive, Jupiter must become a jinn, must make himself invisible at times. Survival also depended on his wearing a mask — a white mask, to cover his Black face. Frantz Fanon, two hundred years later, would know Jupiter Wise as kinfolk. The Dali-esque image "Invitation to Dance," of a figure wearing a white mask and playing a guitar, was ideal; the historical Jupiter Wise not only wore a mask for survival but also held a going away party with music, before he and his comrades fled from slavery. Both "Jupiter Wise" and "Fugitive" show that the enslavement of Africans was part and parcel of life in colonial Canada.

The book moves from historical resilience to contemporary joy. Walking through the streets of Bielefeld, a small German town in Westphalia, the photographer, the poet, and the poet's daughter Lami found Nina Simone on a side street. What a treat! The result, a photo of Lami conversing with the goddess: "Lami and Nina Simone." One woman, a world icon, and the other, coming into the bloom of her womanhood. The poet imagined she heard Nina's voice wailing "To Be Young, Gifted, and Black" during the conversation.

However, when it came time to put text to the photograph, it was not a Westphalian landscape that rose in the poet's mind, but the landscape and seascape of the island of Martinique. In "Lami and Nina," it is in Martinique that the dialectics of the mother–daughter, parent–child bond hit the poet with full force: they are bound together through blood and love forever but are independent of each other at the same time.

In the photo "Women, Metro Station, Lisboa," the photographer captures the aesthetics and pizzazz of the two women waiting for a train in a Lisbon subway station. While the photograph has a playful quality, it also has an unstated shadow side. Portugal was the first European country to initiate the Atlantic Slave Trade from Africa, and the last country to end colonial rule on the continent. Africans in Guinea-Bissau, Angola, and Mozambique fought centuries-old colonial wars against Portugal for their independence. The poem "Queen of Cool" pays homage to the strength, beauty, and sovereignty of African women from antiquity to the present, throughout Africa and its diasporas. Similarly, "Street Musician, Lisboa" is framed by the image of celebrated athlete Mo Farah. The poem it inspired, "Congo Songs: By the Rivers of Babylon, Part Two," is a meditation on diaspora, exile, and loss — but also of triumph, hope, and survival.

In addition to the photographs inspiring the poems, poetry also begat poetry. Sometimes, verses of poems, songs, snatches of phrases, would burst from the poet's subconscious, unconnected to a particular image or photo from the photographer's collection. "A World Greener than Eden" surfaced as she reflected on manhood, work, food, children, slavery, flowers, travel, and love. Appreciating her father's and grandfathers' roles as horticulturalists and providers for their families gave birth to that particular poem. After reading it, the photographer provided "Urban Fields." Though the poet's father planted rural fields, writing the poem from her high-rise building in a very urban setting gave resonance to the photograph. Then, the poet wrote "Uncles," a tribute to all uncles, brothers, sons, dads who must travel far and wide as migrant labourers to work in agro-industries to enrich corporations, but also to reproduce the material lives of their own families. The photographer provided the image "Hoy Aqui — The Suitcase" for "Uncles." It was perfect; uncles must travel to work.

Furthering the theme of love, "Bad Bwoy Jimi" was inspired by the poet's abiding admiration for the guitar and music legend[1] Jimi Hendrix — his music his style, his sheer talent, his vision, his power, and his creative imagination. Knowledge of Jimi's childhood visits to his grandparents in Vancouver contributed vastly to the creation of the poem. The narrator informs Jimi that "ah yuh a fimi" (you are mine) and calls upon legends, history, myths, and Jimi's own grandparents to convince him of her love. The poet uses a form and structure that she hopes captures some aspects of the style of Jimi's music — a kind of rhythm-and-blues rock, driven by up-tempo beats of a riddim guitar and trap drums. The image the photographer provided, "Jimi Hendrix — Composition in Green," shows a transcendental-looking Jimi admired by a lovestruck woman dressed in a green coat.

In "Live with You in a House by the River," the poet invokes nature, culture, art, and music to convey her passion for her spouse. Overcome, she uses an ancient love story, that of Belqis (the Queen of Sheba) and Suleyman (King Solomon) to give her beloved an idea of her love for him. The photographer provided "Woman on Bench," in which the subject's face expresses the longing, desire, and love described in the poem.

Both text and images eventually coalesce around such themes as marronage, parenthood, time travel, grief, fractured ancestry, spiritualities, diasporas, love, resistance, and resilience. In this book, poems and images fuse in their desire to celebrate Blackness as public expression of human relations, aesthetics, and politics.

MAKING BLACKNESS VISIBLE: THE ROLE OF PUBLIC ART

Historical examples of Black performance and art practice in public space inspire our project to document and celebrate Black visibility through urban photography and poetry — its beauty and its power. Art in public, commissioned or trespassing, intervenes in urban development as part of consumer culture and heritage politics. However, public art and artistic practice in public also continue to thrive as expressions of contemporary social and political movements like Black Lives Matter and as agents for turning communal and public spaces into fora for coexistence, environmentalist community, dialogue, participation, and resistance. Art practice continues to break with urban convention, social norms, and spatial configurations, and it does so even more effectively in the high visibility provided by open, accessible, public spaces.

Performance and art practice in public has had a long trajectory in Black cultures from Africa and the American hemisphere. As a frequent traveller between Jamaica and the United States, Marcus Garvey embraced ideas of pan-Africanism and integrated his knowledge of Jamaican and rural traditions from the American South. Arguably, Garvey was the intellectual figure among Black radical thinkers who most enhanced the importance of visibility in public space for the advancement of Black people. Performance in public space was crucial to his politics and aesthetics of change. In parades, public theatre performances, and variety shows in Jamaica and Harlem, Garvey unfolded his performative skills of excess and exploited the subversive potential of multiple sites of cultural production.

To reach a high visibility and audibility in the streets was also central for the politics of the Black Power Movement in the 1960s that fostered identity and community-building in public space. Standing tall in leather jackets and berets, parading in the streets — at times with guns loosely over their shoulders — the Panthers used iconic visibility in public space to establish and secure Black urban structures, including food and medical supplies for the community. From the very beginning of the Panthers, soul musicians articulated and celebrated Black Power in the wake of the Civil Rights Movement and the assassinations of Malcolm X and Martin Luther King. Black sound and iconic Black Power images in streets, parks, and other public sites created a strong Black presence in public sites in cities like Detroit, New York, and Oakland.

The visualization of Black public protest reached a climax with the presumably first Black mural in public space in Chicago in 1967. "Wall of Respect" was an outdoor mural done for the community by a collective of designers, photographers, and artists like the Chicago muralist William Walker. Rather than creating an historical outline of Black cultural and political achievements, the "Wall of Respect" was grouped according to the different kinds of key figures of Black cultures. Rhythm-and-blues and jazz musicians like Aretha Franklin, Billie Holiday, and Miles Davis; political activists such as Harriet Tubman, Marcus Garvey, Malcolm X, and Stokely Carmichael; literary figures such as poet Gwendolyn Brooks; public celebrities as boxer Muhammad Ali; and religious leaders such as Elijah Muhammad ranged side by side on the mural. In their different social spheres and historical times, these figures had expressed their affirmation of and pride in Black cultures. So, all figures depicted on the wall spoke in their own ways to the activism of the Black Power Movement that had spread to Chicago by 1967.

Black Matters, then, is a contemporary dialogue between photographer and poet to make Blackness visible as well as audible.[2] The book pays homage to the cultural, social, and political work that cherishes Black culture, heritage, and resilience. It gratefully reaches out to all street artists that turn public space into a communal setting in which art can be shared freely and, thus, inspire new cultural creativity. Our poems and images are perhaps less spectacular, subtler than the projects of the revolutionaries and artists above.

But like these figures, we desire to extend an awareness of Black presence in contemporary urban space. We aim to do so through revised local histories and an acknowledgement of ongoing, everyday struggles for justice, equality, and peace.

Afua Cooper, Halifax
Wilfried Raussert, Bielefeld

1. For example, see "Love in Lotus Pose," in Afua Cooper, *Copper Woman and Other Poems* (2006)

2. The visibility of Blackness is a subject taken up by many scholars and artists, including Charles Mills. See his *Blackness Visible: Essays on Philosophy and Race* (1998)

BLACK MATTERS

John Ware: Magician Cowboy

They tell us
you brought the longhorn cattle
all the way from Montana to these parts
you rode for a thousand miles

You fled South Carolina to Texas
after slavery ended
Though Blacks were now free
they still had little liberty
White men defeated in the war
could not abide living with emancipated Blacks
instituted racial terror
bloodbaths and lynchings
In Texas you became
a cowboy
working cattle
breaking horses
wrestling steer
answering the call of your totems: horse and cattle

Some say you were born in a saddle
your mama gave birth to you
while escaping slavery on a horse
but they caught her
They say you got the spirit
of the horse
from her
the story is told that before slavery
she was a royal horsewoman from Oyo
Others say it was your father's father
a cattle herder from the African savanna
from whom you received your cow wisdom
They say he travelled for eons with his herd
until he came to the forest kingdom of Osei Tutu
it was there he took the name Owaré

You speak the language of horse and cattle
you can tame any bronco
you calm any wild bull
John Ware
cowboy magician
part of the brotherhood of Black cowboys
who have been erased from the history of the West
From Texas you went to Montana
and then
Alberta
beckoned

Father and Son

A white man named Stimson
wanted you to take a thousand heads of longhorns
to Canada
a territory called the Northwest
still owned by the Hudson's Bay

Canada was a monarchy
not a republic like the one you lived in
a thousand longhorn cattle from Montana
to Alberta

You followed the North Star

John Ware
John Waré
John Owaré
son of the house of Asante
if not for the slave trade
silken Kente would have draped your body
the king would have sent you on diplomatic missions
to Oyo, Gonja, Salaga, Hausa, and Songhai
the symbol of your authority: a cow tail dyed in ochre

With your thousand longhorns
you crossed prairies
scrubland
silent with luminous sadness in your eyes
until you reached Brooks, Alberta
in a new territory that like Oklahoma
was brutally taken
from the original inhabitants
What is the difference between a monarchy and a republic?
you asked yourself

You hated Calgary
and went there only when you must
In Calgary you had to step off the sidewalk
whenever a white person approached
you could not darken the entrance
of any hotel or boardinghouse
Calgary reinforced the shame of your skin
a badge of dishonour
the dishonour and shame you thought
you had left behind in South Carolina and Texas
Only in the wide-open prairies
did you feel truly free

A man must marry
She came from the east
Whitby, Ontario
she had a sensible name — Mildred
she lived with her parents
in Calgary
you visited only twice
before you proposed marriage
she had a good carriage
and a quiet and sure smile

She accepted the offer
you wed
she went with you to your ranch in Brooks
and lived with you among the horses and cattle
Your children
grew up riding horses
and having cows and ponies for pets
later, your two sons would fight
in the Great War

In the early mist of the mornings
you still dream of your mother being whipped
half-naked
her screams waking you up
You hold Mildred close
then ease out of bed
and walk to the children's room
Janet is lying in her crib
dreaming peacefully

Bucking broncos
you must go to Calgary
to participate in cowboy frolic
no one can ride a bronco like you
no wild horse has ever thrown you
In Calgary you showed them
how to tame the feral horses
play with them
put cattle to sleep simply with the vibration of your voice
Your heart work helped to create the
the bacchanal that has become the Calgary stampede
yet your name is written out

The grief of losing Mildred
she died from pneumonia and typhoid
you cry with your motherless children
who knew that loss could hurt so much?

A white man comes to your door
he is rich and famous
he has a horse for you to break
The children tell you not to go
they hang on to your coat
but you owe the white man a favour
and the money is good
You have to support your motherless children

Today is your fifty-fifth birthday
Mildred would have baked you a cake

You go

For the first time in your adult life
a horse throws you
Before you fall
you hold on to its reins
and in cruel fate
your hold has the power
because you are so strong, John
to pull the horse down on you

You look into its blood-filled eyes
feel the breath from its snorting nostrils
his weight is an everlasting mountain
he crushes you

You close your eyes
and your spirit flies
over prairie lands
rice fields and indigo vats
to the forest kingdom
of Osei Tutu
Akwaba Owaré! *
They say your funeral was the biggest
Calgary has ever seen
John Ware
John Owaré
John Waré
John Ware

In Calgary
the newspapers called you the greatest cowboy
who ever lived
horse breaker
steer wrestler
shaman

* Akwaba is from Akan languages. It means "welcome"

FUGITIVE

ELIZABETH RUSSELL SPEAKS OF HER SLAVE PEGGY POMPADOUR

Peggy is in the habit of running away
It would be bad enough
if she left by herself
but now she is taking her children
    with her
She is a very bad woman
a mean slave

She goes to the outskirts of the city
and roams the bushes
eating berries
and wading in the Don River
catching salmon
that still travel to these parts

Diversity, Toronto

She has erected a hut of sorts
from the brambles of the elderberry tree
She lived there with her daughters
Amy and Milly for three weeks
until Peter sent the constables to
   retrieve her
He returned the children to the house
but lodged Peggy in jail

Now he wants to sell her
but neither Joseph Brant
nor Matthew Elliot
wants to buy her
on account of her fugitive career
though they had promised Peter
   they would

Because no one wants her
Peter has to keep her in jail
he resents paying the jailer's fee
If only this mean slave
would behave!

Her so-called husband Pompey
visits her each day
bringing her food, a blanket
and ginger tea
He tells me that even though it is summer
it is still cold in the jail

Once Pompey even snatched the children
from the house to visit her
Pompey is a free man
otherwise we would jail him too

Peggy's incorrigible son Jupiter
has followed in her fugitive steps
He has just run off
someone saw him in the vicinity of
   the Don
around Pottery Road
lurking about Mr. Long's farm
Peter has sent the constables after him

Peter really wishes to be rid of Peggy
I for one do not want her ever again in
    this house
I hate the very sight of her
after she smashed the fine China
I crossed the sea with from Ireland

Because the jailer's fee is mounting
Peter is forced to put an ad in the paper *

Matthew Elliot has disappointed us
Joseph Brant the same
perhaps someone else will take pity
    on Peter
and take the wretch and her son off
    his hand

I have already gifted my goddaughter
    Elizabeth Dennison
with Milly and Amy

TO BE SOLD,
A **BLACK WOMAN**, named PEGGY, aged about forty years ; and a Black boy her son, named JUPITER, aged about fifteen years, both of them the property of the Subscriber.

The Woman is a tolerable Cook and washer woman and perfectly understands making Soap and Candles.

The Boy is tall and strong of his age, and has been employed in Country business, but brought up principally as a House Servant—They are each of them Servants for life. The Price for the Woman is one hundred and fifty Dollars—for the Boy two hundred Dollars, payable in three years with Interest from the day of Sale and to be properly secured by Bond &c.—But one fourth less will be taken in ready Money.

PETER RUSSELL.
York, Feb. 10th 1806.

---

* This historical ad is from the *Upper Canada Gazette*,
  Vol. 15, 45

Invitation to Dance

Jupiter Wise

Arise!
Tell your story
chant your psalm
iqra your chronicle
that of hostile winters
and long sea journeys
read your DNA inscription
Middle Passage survivor

Jupiter Wise
speak of your odyssey
from Boston to Charlottetown
in the sloop that nearly went down
off the coast of Maine
You had no fear
but felt a secret glee
in your heart
as you saw the whites panic
Let them feel the fear of death, for once

And in Charlottetown
you slaved for a master
who called you Jupiter
with full knowledge

that the god was powerful
and you, oh so pitiful

Jupiter
let me see your disguise
play fool fi ketch wise
you with the patoo eyes **
that you use fi hypnotize
white mask, Black skin
tink seh you a jinn

Jupiter Wise
planned a slave escape
across di Northumberland Strait
when dem reach the sea,
dem shout "jubilee"

But they found you
slave master and his crew
found you
took you to the hanging tree
and you plead the benefit of clergy

The judges spared your life
warned you about causing strife
sentenced you to West Indian slavery
but you escaped to Nova Scarcity
lived there as a Maroon with your wife

A fighting slave
you quested for your freedom
in your head you heard the jubilee drum
Jupiter Wise
don your disguise
white mask, Black skin
rock and come in

*   Jupiter Wise was an enslaved man who in 1785 sought to free
    himself from Prince Edward Island slavery
** Patoo in African Jamaican language is an owl

UNCLES

Uncles cut cane on Louisiana plantations
wore knee-high, steel-toe boots
to keep their feet and legs safe
from poisonous snakes
that slithered through the fields
Uncles labouring under hot sun
man did tink seh slavery done

Hoy Aqui — The Suitcase

Uncles grow oranges on Florida orchards
spray the seedlings with a substance
that burns their skin
And once the oranges dem full-full
they pack them in crates that reach the sky
Man sweat for penny wages, tink him gwine die

Uncles have been travelling and toiling for a long time
They often think of home
of their mothers making them chocolatetea *
and fry fish and bammie
of teaching their nieces to ride bicycles
sitting on verandahs with their wives eating popsicles

* Chocolate is the ground form of cocoa or cacao

Shots Rang Out on My Street Today

Boyakka! Boyakka! Boyakka!
Boyakka! Boyakka! Boyakka!
Boyakka! Boyakka! Boyakka!

Shots rang out on my street today
three Black yoots lay dead
shot inna dem head

And dem madda ban har belly an bawl
And dem madda ban har belly an bawl

Boyakka! Boyakka! Boyakka!

Black Uhuru did seh
di yoots of Eglington
won't put down dem Remington
di yoots of Brixton they have their
    45 Smith & Wesson *

But I Afua Cooper seh,
di yoots of Halifax won't put down
    dem scorpion
di yoots of Dartmut
well familiar wid dem glock

Annada one die inna di miggle passage
Annada one lost inna di miggle passage

And mammy ban har belly an bawl
And mammy ban har belly an bawl

Here in Halifax
some call it Hellafacts
capital of Nova Scotia
New Caledonia
New Scotland
Albion-ia

Atlanta Airport

Halifax
the shiny white city on the hill
the promised land
the New Jerusalem
our children die
we ask why

As a madda ban har belly an bawl
As a madda ban har belly an bawl

The pastor cry out loud
"peace in the East
put down the guns,
save our sisters and sons"
The police chief seh
"arrest is not the ansa,
we have to get to the root of the matter"
The social worker step up
"we know the ansa
it is social isolation
educational marginalization
economic deprivation
that is the cause of this situation
time to write another dissertation"

No, we do not want this new Jerusalem
let us step up into Mount Zion
Zion train is coming our way! **

Black Uhuru seh
di yoots of Eglington
won't put down dem Remington
di yoots of Brixton they have their
   45 Smith & Wesson
And I Afua Cooper seh
di yoots of Halifax won't put down
   dem scorpion
di yoots of Dartmut
carry dem gun beneath dem shut

How dem get the guns?
How dem get the guns?
Canada has gun control
how dem get the guns?

Shots rang out on my street today
three Black yoots lay dead
shot inna dem head

Annada one killed inna di miggle passage
Annada one murdered inna di miggle passage
Annada one died inna di miggle passage
And mammy ban har belly an bawl,
and mammy ban har belly an bawl!
Mammy ban har belly an bawl

She seh
"mi wash belly
mi only pickney
mi wash belly"

Shots rang out on my street today
three Black yoots lay dead
shot inna dem head

Boyakka! Boyakka! Boyakka!
Boyakka! Boyakka! Boyakka!
Boyakka! Boyakka! Boyakka!

* "Youths of Eglington" is a song by Black Uhuru
** "Zion Train" is a song by Bob Marley

WHAT DO YOU DO WITH THE HURT?

What do you do with the hurt?
Do you fold it neatly and tuck it
in a dark corner of your closet
Do you drag it around like bag and pan
or lead it around like a weeping child?

What do you do with the hurt?
Weep with it as you both listen
to Mozart's sad arias
sung by Kathleen Battle

What do you do with the hurt?
Lie in bed and force it to be quiet
get some sleep

What do you do with the hurt?
Run a half marathon
spend hours on the treadmill
until the gym trainer tells you
you are overdoing it

What do you do with the hurt?
Swallow it?
Force yourself to digest it?
Pray to eliminate it?

What do you do with the hurt?
Your husband calls you a witch
when you tell him his woman's hair salon
is painted pink
and that she has six fingers on her left hand

You watch his face contort
as he hisses "witch!
How do you know that?
You've never met her!"

And you tell him, you saw it in a dream

Looking in Different Directions

What do you do with the hurt?
Call up his mistress
the mother of his illegitimate child
and she might tell you that
she too has a hurt
and does not know what to do with it

What do you do with the hurt?
Write a poem as you sit on the bus
#22 from Mumford terminal to Peggy's Cove

What do you do with the hurt?

Breathe
release
let go?

Or sit on that huge rock in the river
that flows from Albayzín
open your arms to the sun
let its rays warm your chest
caress your breasts
animate your heart
feel the hurt grow smaller

FOR POETRY'S SAKE: THE FOUR SEASONS

Caught in the grip of winter
I no longer slump in the aisles of the library and weep
while thinking of sunny isles
I merely look winter in the face and say
"poetry shall deal with you"

Woman Approaching the Wall
- Sigrid

Then spring gives birth to me,
I am young again
waiting to be scorched by the summer
A summer in whose arms I lie,
a summer to whom I erect altars
so that he may not go away
but remain with me forever

But like all hot affairs, it ends
and I am left alone to face the fall

A fall that reveals its shimmering beauty
a beauty that comes covered in a shroud
Caught in this deception
I long for summer
but autumn laughs with golden teeth
and instructs me to write
"You are a poet," he says,
"you are a poet"

CIMARRON

I sit at the edge of the Alhambra
below me the world is as flat as a map
the plains go on forever
at their edges I see the foothills of
    the Sierra Nevada
and over those mountains are Sevilla
    and Cordoba
Oh Andalucía!

The sun is setting over Granada
The world is still for a brief moment
held in the embrace of orange translucence
The great fireball pulled by Arabian steeds
hurries toward the west

The voice of the gypsy
echoes all over Albayzín and Sacromonte
and in his voice I hear
Boabdil's last sigh

To my right
from the mosque
the muezzin sings the adhan
proclaiming maghrib
the sunset prayer
And behind me is San Nícolas cathedral
(it used to be the grand mosque before
    the conquista)
and it will soon ring its bells
announcing vespers

Night comes suddenly
and the neighbourhood awakens
Flamenco dancers, men and
    women, arrive
they dance, their heels
clicking on the cobbled stones
enlivened by gitano singers

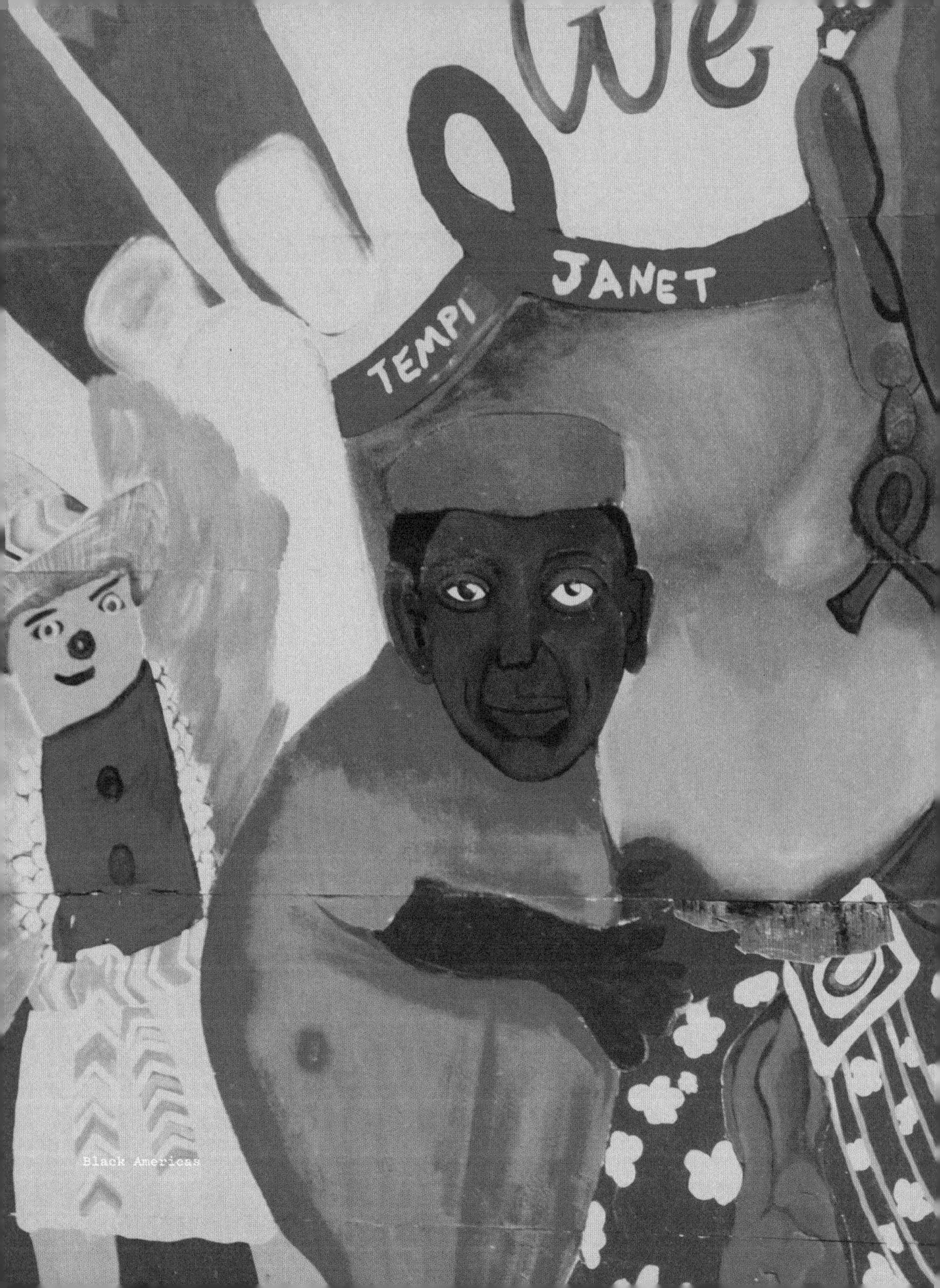

Black Americas

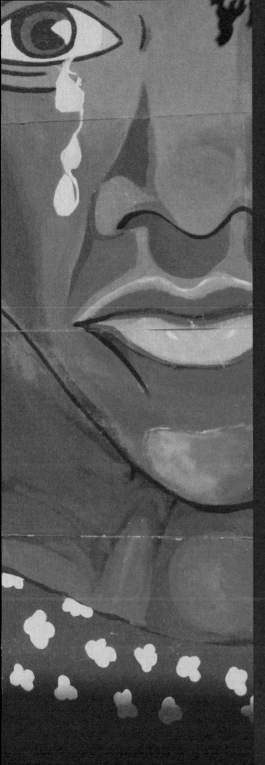

Tourists crowd around
clapping and cheering
I join, imitating the movement
   of the dancers

A youth comes to me
and shows me the bracelets he is selling
I made them myself, three for ten euros
he looks at me intently
you look like my sister

I am from Mexico, he said
Veracruz
I am Black like you
Do you know of Yanga?
I am Black like him
I am a Cimarron like him

GUADALAJARA STREET

If I were to die and come back reborn
it would be as a poet
says the Rasta child on Guadalajara street
but his cans of paint and the graffitied wall
behind him
declare him a painter

If I were to die and come back reborn
it would be as a poet

He has no choice
of course he would come back a poet
he lives in the city of the painter-poet
the electric painter
the one named José Clemente Orozco
Ever seen his painting, *Man of Fire?*
I have
At the Hospicio Cabañas
set in the middle of the ceiling
the fury of red hot lava
spilling from his entrails

Don't Think Twice, It's All Right *

Don't think twice, it's all right
It's all right little man
It's all right

You will have your music to carry you through
through this journey called life
and you will have your smile too
your smile bright as a thousand Teotihuacan sunrise

And you will have your papa too
little man
your papa wise as the morning sun
your papa strong and sturdy like a tree

Don't think twice, it's all right

* "Don't Think Twice, It's All Right" is a
  song by Bob Dylan

Welcome by Bob Dylan

LAMI AND NINA

How my love for you at this moment
is so sweet and sad,
girl of my dreams
woman of my heart
you with the eyes of eternal beauty

Standing at the departure gate at
    Aimé Césaire airport at Lamentin
I said to myself, "another departure"
The children have grown up
the ancient hearth has been disrupted
it is the circle of life
I, too, have left my mother
created, like Hagar and Hathor, my
    own house
with my own children
my own husband
my own fireplace
my own vineyard
my own journey between Safa and Marwa
as you will too, one day

Music bursts from speakers hidden
    in walls
it is Nina Simone

To be young, gifted, and Black
Oh, what a lovely precious dream *

But I am proud of you
and your womanly ways,
your smartness and intelligence
your kindness and humility
your joie de vivre
your light and colour
your music
your love of the water
your commitment to knowledge

Will we ever live together again?
We ask each other,
will the hearth be reconstituted?
You are so optimistic
and in your light, airy, and colourful way
you say, "yes, of course, but we will have
    two homes"

Now I know that everything has a season,
a lifespan
Truly, wisdom comes with age
But knowing that I still mourn
for our house that was, and is now gone
the life we used to live and share
as mother and daughter
as parent and daughter
as sister to sister

What pleasure I used to take in
    preparing your food from scratch,
no store-bought baby food for you
the blender was my best friend
Teaching you to read and count
teaching you your colours
taking you to baby swim lessons
baby music class

Putting you in your stroller and
taking you to the park and the
    wading pool
how you delighted in water!
Singing to you
and playing you music from Phyllis
    Dillon to Chopin
to Babatunde Olatunji and
    Kathleen Battle

Your plane will pass my building
on its way to the open sea
I sit on the verandah
in the neighbourhood close to Texaco
to wait

Lami and Nina Simone

It will fly across the harbour,
(this beautiful stretch of sea
with Fort-de-France on one side
and Pointe du Bout and Les Trois-Îlets
    on the other
When God was creating harbours
she chose this one as the diadem)
in the direction of St-Pierre
Then it will head north toward
    La Dominique
and Guadeloupe, and then climb higher
    and higher
in the sky until it flies over Puerto Rico
and heads toward the open Atlantic
passing glittering cities
Miami, Charleston, Philadelphia
New York, Boston
Then it will skirt toward the West
over Vermont
and on to Montréal
From that great river port
you will take another plane to Toronto
the great Great Lakes destination
our emotional home

I will not sleep
until I get a text saying you
arrived at Pearson and you are on your
    way home

We knew each other
even before you were created in my womb
my daughter of light years
We held hands across centuries
and trekked across continents
until one Sunday morning in February
in Toronto
(the temperature was minus
    eleven degrees)
you landed on my bed and waved hello

The sun will soon set over this
diadem of a harbour
and I will go to my room
and perhaps write in my diary
or do my French homework
or sit and gaze at the Caribbean Sea
that lies majestically in front of
    my building

This sea of history
this sea on which my ancestors trekked
in their captivity
the sea on whose shores I was born
and where my navel string was buried
the sea over which you now fly
this sea that changes its colours every
    fifteen minutes
Gazing at the sea
is a long contemplation

Daughter of my heart
continuation of my hearth
you with the twinkling eyes
and your Belqis of Axum cheekbones
your teeth like pearls from the south
    Caribbean Sea

There's a world waiting for you
Yours is a quest that's just begun

When you're young, gifted, and Black
Your soul's intact! *

---

* "To Be Young, Gifted, and Black" is a song
by Nina Simone that was considered to be
an anthem of the Civil Rights Movement

THINGS *I* LIKE DOING

TO THE MEMORY OF NAZIM HIKMET

I like doing laundry and folding the clothes
making green drinks and blue smoothies
riffing on old recipes created
by my grandmother Georgiana Vanhorn
Hanging out with my grandsons
teaching them to read
and playing word games
Poking my head into old churches
looking at the stained-glass windows
the Church of the Holy Trinity
and Our Lady of Perpetual Help
are my favourites
Zikhr-ing early in the morning
feeling the names echoing in my bones
thinking about what my grandfather Neil Campbell
    looked like
they say he was tall and thin
Looking at murals by Alfaro and Orozco
reading Monet's biography
and Kamau Brathwaite's poems
Standing with you by the Christmas tree
decorating it with red, white, and green balls
thinking: "how can I win your love?"

Christmas Romance

Woman on Bench

LIVE WITH YOU IN A HOUSE BY THE RIVER

I want to live with you in a house by the river

fall asleep in your arms, hushed by the gurgling sound

of water

wake up in the morning and roast breadfruit

and cook rundown for your breakfast

play you love songs on my lute

You will grow lilies and morning glory

at the bottom of the steps that lead to the verandah

You will line the footpath with red and white roses

You will colour our cottage

with blue and gold from a Haitian painting

And best of all, you will build for me the marriage bed

the headboard decorated with cooing doves

I love you like Belqis love Suleyman

My love, come recline with me

round my belly with generations of your children

YOU DANCE

Lawd, look di way you dance
you dance

       you dance

        you dance

You hold up your head
square your shoulders
all rigid-like
den you get loose
an start to shake
Lawd, look di way you dance
dance
dance
dance

It's like when you dance
something in you, like a dam

Urban Dance: New Orleans

burst open and start to flow
and you just dance, dance, dance, and
    dance
you dance with the wind
for the wind
against the wind
Your hands held high in supplication
to God
you dance
Now, it's like Damballah possess you
your body start rippling like a snake
undulating like the waves
seductive as the sea
the woman of the ocean in you
as you dance
dance
dance
dance
But now your body is contorting
you bend over in pain
lawd, you must be dying
But look! You come to life again
and dance
                dance
                    dance

Chile, is who fah pickney is you
who you belong to
who initiate you
into the rites of Vodou
where you learn fi dance so
fi dance so
fi dance so?

Look di way you dance!

BAD BWOY JIMI

Bad bwoy Jimi
ah yuh a fimi
me is yuh Black Madonna
the one named Ava Maria

Bad bwoy Jimi
come an getti
love along di watchtower
guitar caress ur purple flower

Bad bwoy Jimi
it's ur girl from Hogan's Alley
the love of ur life
the island wife

Bad bwoy Jimi
Ross and Nora betrothed us as baby *
sea horn across the Georgia Straight
announced you as my eternal mate

Choctaw fighter
assegai thrower
merman
Black panther!

*   Ross and Nora were Jimi Hendrix's
    grandparents; they lived in Vancouver
    where he spent time during his
    childhood

Jimi Hendrix-Composition in

Women, Metro Station, Lisboa

QUEEN OF COOL

U 2 cool
Rift Valley sista
ruler of all the lands of the Nile
empress of Kush
double Afrodite
Lisbon worships at your feet

SEE-FAR WOMAN

When Olorun created the Earth
she pulled the poles apart
separated the East from the West
blessed humans with four eyes
gifting them with the ability
to look and see in every direction

Kensedeobong Blessed
Okosun–The Photographer

A World Greener Than Eden

MY FATHER PLANTED A PROVISION GROUND

My father planted a provision ground
with yams of all sorts
yellow
white
Negro
afu
Lucea
even yampee
and sweet potatoes
with red skin
golden skin
white skin
and pumpkins
squash
dasheen
baddus
coco
cassava

cucumber
and other root and vine crops
gungo peas
okras
plantains
and bananas
He planted breadfruit
and ackee trees
and like the agronomist he was
crafted a tree
that bore June plum,
avocado, and jackfruit at the same time

For the short term
dad planted a callaloo patch
with pap chow *
spinach
bell peppers
bird peppers
scotch bonnet
carrots
garlic
onions
scallions

My father always praised the soil

* Pap chow is Jamaican for bok choy

Decades before,

my grandfather planted citrus groves

with sweet orange

Seville orange

tangerine

lime

the startling lemon

and grapefruit trees that,

every season,

bore so much

that neighbours

friends, and passersby

invited themselves into our yard to partake

Grandfather also planted coconut trees

made his own oil and milk from the coconut flesh

grew sugarcane

had his own mill that pressed

the juice from the cane

made wet sugar

and molasses

tended a cocoa walk

from which he prepared chocolate

to make chocolatetea

which he sweetened with the wet sugar

and flavoured with coconut milk,

nutmeg, and cinnamon powder for us

Grandfather also planted corn

These men built a well,

with a spout pointing

in each of the four directions,

that carried water
to irrigate
the crops they planted

Urban Fields

CONGO SONGS: BY THE RIVERS OF BABYLON, PART TWO

We gonna sing Congo songs
inna Babylon this morning

Congo songs
Congo songs

And they won't be songs of grief and exile
won't be songs of pain and sorrow
Congo songs

Congo songs inna Babylon this morning
Congo songs

They won't be songs of trouble and trial
Congo songs
won't be songs of heartbreak and misery
Congo songs

MO FARAH
MEDALHA DE OURO OLÍMPICA: 5000M / 1000

Street Musician, Lisboa

But songs of joy and laughter
Congo songs
songs of strength and sunshine
Congo songs

Songs of children bawning
Congo songs
songs of mothers birthing
Congo songs

Songs of grandmothers living
and of fathers breathing
Congo songs

No more songs of agony and anguish
No more songs of woe and calamity

We gonna sing Congo songs

Songs of brothers striding
songs of sisters striving
songs of grandfathers dancing

We gonna sing Congo songs

No more songs of children dying
but of the sun arising
Congo songs

Songs of the certainty of us living

songs of the certainty of us living
songs of mothers birthing
songs of children singing

We gonna sing Congo songs
inna Babylon this morning
Congo songs
Congo songs